MILITARY AIRCRAFT

A-10 THUNDERBOLT II

BY JOHN HAMILTON

VISIT US AT
WWW.ABDOPUBLISHING.COM

Published by ABDO Publishing Company, PO Box 398166, Minneapolis, MN 55439.
Copyright ©2013 by Abdo Consulting Group, Inc. International copyrights reserved in all
countries. No part of this book may be reproduced in any form without written permission
from the publisher. A&D Xtreme™ is a trademark and logo of ABDO Publishing Company.

Printed in the United States of America, North Mankato, Minnesota.
082012
012013

 PRINTED ON RECYCLED PAPER

Editor: Sue Hamilton
Graphic Design: Sue Hamilton
Cover Design: John Hamilton
Cover Photo: U.S. Air Force
Interior Photos: All photos United States Air Force except: Department of Defense-pgs 22
& 24-25; Getty Images-pg 23; United States Navy-pgs 10-11.

ABDO Booklinks
Web sites about Military Aircraft are featured on our Book Links pages. These links are
routinely monitored and updated to provide the most current information available. Web
site: www.abdopublishing.com

Cataloging-in-Publication Data

Hamilton, John, 1959-
 A-10 Thunderbolt II / John Hamilton.
   p. cm. -- (Xtreme military aircraft set 2)
Includes index.
ISBN 978-1-61783-685-5
1. A-10 (Jet attack plane)--Juvenile literature. 2. Airplanes,
Military--United States--Juvenile literature. I. Title.
623.74--dc15

                                    2012946022

TABLE OF CONTENTS

A-10 ★ ★ ★ THUNDERBOLT II

The A-10 Thunderbolt II is a fighter jet flown by the United States Air Force. It is a deadly aircraft used to support ground troops and destroy enemy tanks.

Three A-10 Thunderbolt II aircraft fly in formation during a training exercise. Able to take off from short runways, the nimble A-10 operates near the front lines. When American and allied ground troops need help, an A-10 can get to the battlefield quickly.

XTREME FACT

An A-10 Thunderbolt can prowl around the battlefield for long periods of time, even in bad weather or at night.

MISSION: CLOSE AIR SUPPORT

Helping friendly ground forces is the A-10 Thunderbolt II's most important job. It is the only piloted aircraft built just for this mission, which is called "close air support." The A-10 can fly over the battlefield for hours. When friendly troops need air support, the A-10 is ready to strike.

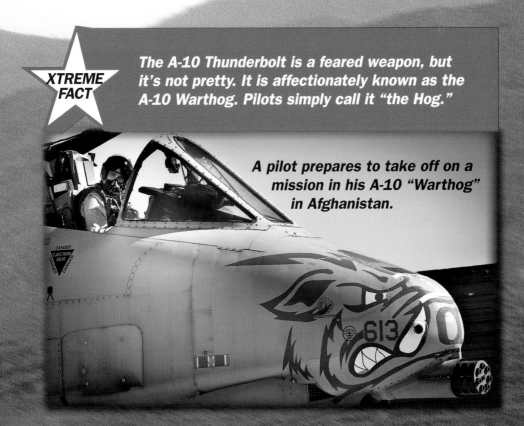

The A-10 Thunderbolt is a feared weapon, but it's not pretty. It is affectionately known as the A-10 Warthog. Pilots simply call it "the Hog."

A pilot prepares to take off on a mission in his A-10 "Warthog" in Afghanistan.

The A-10 is one of the
United States military's
deadliest weapons.
It is known as a
"tankbuster." It flies
"low and slow," making
it easier for A-10 pilots
to spot tanks. Even
though it looks clunky,
the aircraft can make
quick turns and swoop
in to attack. The A-10
can even fly at night, or
during bad weather.

On attack runs, A-10s fly at an altitude between 100 to 300 feet (30 to 91 m), at a maximum speed of about 340 miles per hour (547 kph).

A-10 aircraft fly over a Soviet T-62A tank. Thunderbolt IIs are known as "tankbusters," with the ability to fly low enough and slow enough to take out heavily armed fighting vehicles.

OTHER MISSIONS

A-10 Thunderbolt IIs are sometimes used in "forward air control" missions. Because they fly slowly and have a good view of the battlefield, A-10s can direct other planes to attack the enemy.

A-10s are also sometimes used in search-and-rescue missions. When a friendly plane is shot down, A-10s can fly over the crash site and help special operations troops bring the crew safely home.

An A-10 Thunderbolt II takes off, flying low above a tree line.

ORIGINS

In the late 1960s, during the Vietnam War, the United States Air Force began developing a new aircraft. Its sole mission was to defend friendly ground troops better than existing aircraft or helicopters.

The A-10 Thunderbolt II was chosen to fill this important role. The first A-10 was delivered to the United States Air Force in 1975. Today, the Air Force flies nearly 200 active-duty A-10s.

One of the first A-10 Thunderbolt IIs arrives at Langley Air Force Base in Virginia in 1976.

XTREME FACT

The A-10 Thunderbolt II is named after the P-47 Thunderbolt, a famous fighter-bomber aircraft flown during World War II.

A-10 Thunderbolt II
Fast
Facts

A-10 Thunderbolt II Specifications

Function:	Close air support
Service Branch:	United States Air Force
Manufacturer:	Fairchild Republic
Crew:	One
Length:	53 feet, 4 inches (16.3 m)
Height:	14 feet, 8 inches (4.5 m)
Wingspan:	57 feet, 6 inches (17.5 m)

A-10 Thunderbolt IIs can take so much
punishment that they can fly even if
half a wing is completely destroyed!

Maximum Takeoff
  Weight: **51,000 pounds (23,133 kg)**
Cruising Speed: **340 miles per hour (547 kph)**
Ceiling: **45,000 feet (13,716 m)**
Combat Range: **2,240 nautical miles**
                    (2,578 miles, or 4,149 km)

THE AVENGER CANNON

The A-10 Thunderbolt II is built around its most powerful weapon, the GAU-8/A Avenger Gatling-type cannon. The Avenger was originally built to destroy tanks. It can also be used against trucks, bunkers, or other enemy targets.

An A-10 Thunderbolt II test fires its nose-mounted GAU-8/A Avenger 30mm seven-barrel cannon.

The Avenger has seven barrels arranged on a cylinder. It rotates at high speed. It fires 30mm armor-piercing shells at a rate of about 3,900 rounds per minute, or 65 rounds per second.

XTREME FACT

The GAU-8/A Avenger is almost 20 feet (6 m) long, and weighs about 4,000 pounds (1,814 kg) fully loaded.

A cutaway drawing of a GAU-8/A Avenger cannon used on the Thunderbolt II aircraft.

17

Each round of 30mm ammunition fired by the Avenger weighs 1.53 pounds (.7 kg) and measures 11.4 inches (29 cm) long.

The GAU-8/A Avenger is mounted inside the front fuselage of the A-10 Thunderbolt II. It holds about 1,200 rounds of ammunition. To strafe enemy ground forces, the A-10 goes into a dive. The pilot lines up the front of the plane with the target. When the Avenger fires, the whole plane shakes. The loud, low-frequency "growl" can be heard on the ground. It is a frightening sound to enemy infantry.

The Avenger is very accurate, even at long range. It does devastating damage to the enemy. When friendly forces are in trouble, they are always happy to see Warthogs come to the rescue.

OTHER WEAPONS

The A-10 Thunderbolt II can carry several kinds of missiles and bombs under its wings. The AGM-65 Maverick is an air-to-surface missile. It destroys enemy tanks at a longer range than the Avenger cannon. Cluster bombs contain dozens of smaller bomblets. They are designed to kill enemy infantry or destroy light vehicles. The A-10 is also usually armed with two AIM-9 Sidewinder air-to-air missiles. They are used to defend against enemy aircraft.

An A-10 drops an AGM-65 Maverick missile during a training mission.

The upgraded A-10C version of the Thunderbolt II includes laser- or GPS-guided "smart" bombs and missiles.

A pilot fires a missile from his A-10 Thunderbolt II in a live-fire training mission over the Pacific Alaska Range Complex near Eielson Air Force Base in Alaska.

COCKPIT

The A-10 Thunderbolt II is flown by a single pilot. The cockpit is located at the front of the aircraft. A large bubble canopy gives the pilot a good view of the battlefield. The canopy is made of bullet-resistant glass. Under the canopy, the cockpit is surrounded by thick titanium armor. This enclosure is called a "bathtub." It protects the pilot from bullets or explosives.

A pilot sits in the cockpit as his plane is refueled during a combat situation practice.

The cockpit is made of bullet-resistant glass and titanium to protect the pilot in a battle.

Inside the cockpit of an A-10 Thunderbolt II.

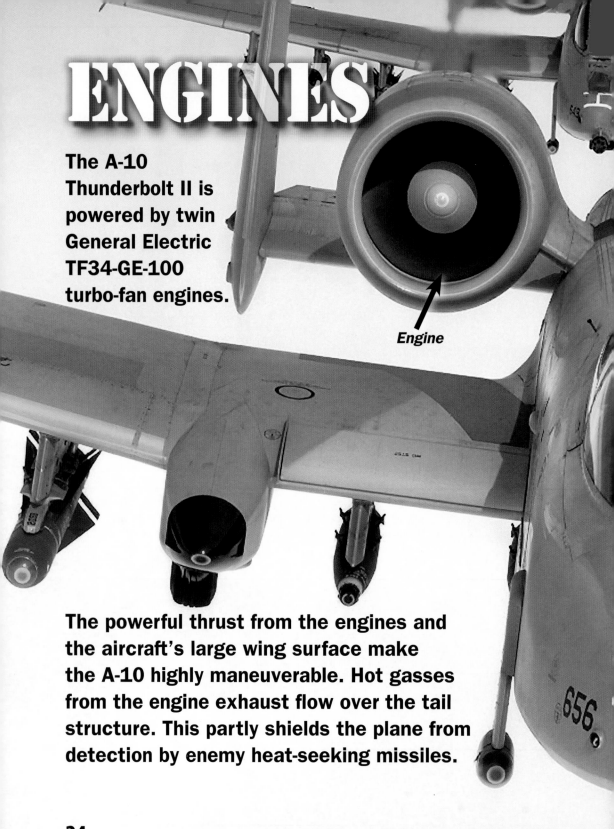

ENGINES

The A-10 Thunderbolt II is powered by twin General Electric TF34-GE-100 turbo-fan engines.

Engine

The powerful thrust from the engines and the aircraft's large wing surface make the A-10 highly maneuverable. Hot gasses from the engine exhaust flow over the tail structure. This partly shields the plane from detection by enemy heat-seeking missiles.

XTREME FACT

The A-10 Thunderbolt II can fly home safely on just one of its two engines if one is destroyed by enemy fire.

Engine

The A-10's engines are mounted on the main fuselage just above and behind the wings.

SURVIVABILITY

Because they fly so slow and close to the battlefield, A-10 Thunderbolt IIs are designed to be tough. They can suffer tremendous damage and keep flying.

Two A-10s from Alaska's Eielson Air Force Base fly over mountainous terrain. Thunderbolts are made to survive battle and weather extremes.

Warthogs can survive direct hits from enemy armor-piercing or explosive shells. Fuel cells are self-sealing when punctured by bullets or shrapnel. If hydraulic flight controls are damaged, A-10s have manual mechanical backups so pilots can fly home safely.

COMBAT HISTORY

The A-10 Thunderbolt II first proved its worth in the Middle East in 1991 during Operation Desert Storm. Also in the 1990s, A-10s were flown during conflicts in Bosnia and Herzegovina, and Kosovo. Starting in 2002, A-10 Thunderbolt IIs played a critical role in the U.S.-led wars in Iraq and Afghanistan. Allied troops fighting Taliban and al-Qaeda forces depended on close air support supplied by Warthogs.

An A-10 Thunderbolt II deploys flares over Afghanistan in 2008.

The A-10 Thunderbolt II may eventually be replaced by a high-tech multirole fighter such as the F-35 Lightning II. However, the United States Air Force plans to use its fleet of Warthogs for many years to come.

XTREME FACT

During Operation Desert Storm, Warthogs destroyed more than 900 Iraqi tanks.

GLOSSARY

ALLIED FORCES
Nations that are allied, or joined, in a fight against a common enemy.

ARMOR
A strong, protective covering made to protect military vehicles.

FUSELAGE
The main body of a plane.

GPS (GLOBAL POSITIONING SYSTEM)
A system of orbiting satellites that transmits information to GPS receivers on Earth. Using information from the satellites, receivers can calculate location, speed, and direction with great accuracy.

INFANTRY
Soldiers who move and fight mainly on foot.

MULTIROLE
Able to perform more than one task or mission. Multirole aircraft can attack enemy targets in the air or on land.

NAUTICAL MILE
A standard way to measure distance, especially when traveling in an aircraft or ship. It is based on the circumference of the Earth, the distance around the equator. This large circle is divided into 360 degrees. Each degree is further divided into 60 units called "minutes." A single minute of arc around the Earth is one nautical mile.

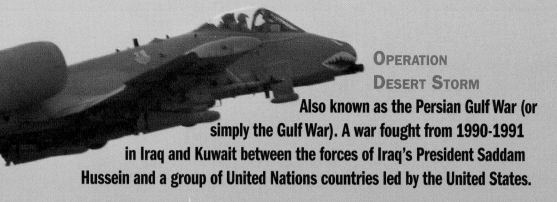

Operation Desert Storm

Also known as the Persian Gulf War (or simply the Gulf War). A war fought from 1990-1991 in Iraq and Kuwait between the forces of Iraq's President Saddam Hussein and a group of United Nations countries led by the United States.

Shrapnel

A deadly fragment of a bomb that flies through the air after the explosion.

Smart Bomb

Precision-guided weapons, also called "smart bombs," are bombs or missiles that can be steered in mid-air toward their targets. They are guided by lasers, radar, or satellite signals.

Strafe

When low-flying aircraft attack objects on the ground, usually with rapid-firing weapons. A-10 Thunderbolt IIs use a GAU-8/A Avenger Gatling-type cannon mounted in their nose to strafe ground targets.

Titanium

A silver-gray metal that is lightweight yet very hard and strong.

Turbo-Fan Engine

A jet engine that gets extra thrust from a turbine-driven fan.

Vietnam War

A conflict between the countries of North Vietnam and South Vietnam from 1955–1975. Communist North Vietnam was supported by China and the Soviet Union. The United States entered the war on the side of South Vietnam.

INDEX